Read-Aloud Plays

Tall Tales

by Carol Pugliano-Martin

SCHOLASTIC
PROFESSIONAL BOOKS

New York • Toronto • London • Auckland • Sydney
Mexico City • New Delhi • Hong Kong

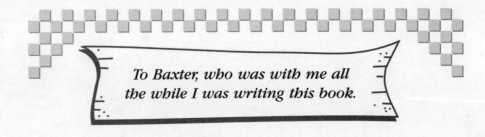

To Baxter, who was with me all the while I was writing this book.

For information regarding permission, write to Scholastic Professional Books, 555 Broadway, New York, NY 10012.

Cover art by Kristin Barr

Cover design by Norma Ortiz

Interior art by Paulette Bogan, Delana Bettoli, and Mike Moran

Interior design by Sydney Wright

ISBN: 0-439-11367-9

Copyright © 2000 by Carol Pugliano-Martin

All rights reserved.

Printed in the U.S.A.

Contents

Introduction

Since the beginning of time, people have told stories. From the earliest cave drawings to the sophisticated cinematography of today, generations of story-tellers have embarked on voyages of fantasy and truth and preserved glimpses of history through legends that have spanned centuries, cultures, and locations.

Like most countries, the United States has a rich treasure trove of stories that reveal its heritage and spirit. Some of the most fun and interesting of these are called tall tales. Tall tales are exaggerated stories of larger-than-life heroes per-forming amazing feats. In his book *Children and Their Literature* (Prentice-Hall, 1988), Professor Constantine Georgiou of New York University describes the tall tale hero as one who "... embodies the cultural characteristics of his native back-ground as well as the abstract qualities of goodness, courage, and cleverness."

With all this wrapped up in one genre, tall tales continue to have an important influence on children's manner of thinking and historical understanding. Studying America's tall tales is also a great way for students to learn about the geography of our nation, and they're a lot of fun to read!

In this book you will find eight plays that bring tall tales to life. These plays offer students opportunities to be heroes—to put themselves in the shoes of early settlers and feel larger than life as they act out adventures of extraordinary characters. You'll also find background information on each tale and engaging extension activities that integrate writing, language arts, social studies, math, science, and art.

As I write this introduction, I am expecting my first child, a son. Like most, if not all parents-to-be, I have hopes and dreams for the kind of person he will become. I hope that he will embody the kindness of Johnny Appleseed; the self-confidence of Sally Ann Thunder Ann Whirlwind; the strength and perseverance of John Henry, Annie Christmas, and Stormalong; and the ingenuity of Febold Feboldson, Paul Bunyan, Pecos Bill, and Slue-Foot Sue.

I also hope that your students will learn from the characters in these timeless tales and revel in their fun, adventure, and self-confidence.

—*Carol Pugliano-Martin*

Activities to Use With
Tall Tale Plays

The following activities offer ways to compare, contrast, and extend the tall tale plays in this book. They can be used with all or any of the plays.

Language Arts

What Is a Tall Tale? Before reading any of the plays in this book, introduce the topic of tall tales to your students. Ask students if they know what a tall tale is. If they need help, tell them that the name provides a clue. Then explain that tall tales are stories that use exaggeration—the characters and their actions might be based on real events, but they are exaggerated to make an incredible story that is more interesting and entertaining. Let students practice writing sentences that include exaggeration. On the chalkboard, write sentence starters such as "My cat is so big, _____."

Ask students to complete the sentence with their own ideas (she uses a swimming pool for a water bowl; her purr can be heard in China; and so on). Let students come up with other sentence starters for classmates to complete.

Compare Characters Chart similarities and differences among the characters, settings, and circumstances of different tall tales. How many characters are known for their enormous size? Their wisdom? What problems do characters face, and how do they solve them? Which plays rely on metaphor and simile to make a point? With what elements of nature do the characters interact? See the sample chart below.

Adventures With Water

Who	What	Where
Stormalong	wrestled a giant octopus	off the New England coast
Annie Christmas	pulled keelboat to safety	Mississippi River
Febold Feboldson	used frogs to bring rain	Great Plains
Slue-Foot Sue	rode a giant catfish; lassoed the Big and Little Dippers to bring rain	Texas
Paul Bunyan	straightened a river with Babe's help	Minnesota

Create a Hero As a class, create your own tall tale hero. Brainstorm with students a list of characteristics—physical, intellectual, and emotional. Where does the character live? What was her childhood like? What does she look like? (size, clothing, voice, hair color, and so on) What are her skills? What amazing feats can she perform? Help students write and illustrate their own tall tale plays, starring their character.

Tell It Like It Is! Tall tales offer endless opportunities to play with and explore language. Help students find and identify slang terms in the plays and replace them with their true meanings. Retell parts of a story or add extra scenes, maintaining tone and character.

Dramatic Arts and Music

Bring Words to Life Have students dramatize the plays by acting them out or using puppets. Record the drama on videotape or audiocassette.

Imitate Art Let students choose instruments (or create their own) to represent the characters in tall tale plays. For example, they might represent Paul Bunyan walking through the woods by banging on a drum (or a trash can turned upside down). Have them play the appropriate instruments each time the characters appear.

Social Studies

Where Did They Go? On a United States map, help students find and mark Minnesota, Pennsylvania, and other locations in which the tall tales take place. Provide colored yarn in a variety of colors. Let students use a different color to represent each character and pin it to the map to track the travels of different characters.

Math

How Many? Make a math activity out of any tall tale. For example, how many pancakes would Paul Bunyan's cook have been able to make at one time? Plot out a pan as big as a skating rink in the school yard or gymnasium. Then place several paper pancakes on the "griddle" and determine how many fit in a designated space. Have students work together to multiply their figures and estimate the number of pancakes one might cook at one time on a griddle this size.

Science

Spin-Offs in Science Extend the science concepts in the tall tales. Have students plant seeds to honor Johnny Appleseed; study weather with Stormalong, Febold Feboldson, and Annie Christmas; or study the constellations and other celestial objects with Pecos Bill and Slue Foot Sue.

Resources

American Tall Tales by Mary Pope Osborne (Knopf, 1991). Johnny Appleseed, Stormalong, and Sally Ann Thunder Ann Whirlwind are just some of the tall tale heroes featured in this excellent collection.

The Bunyans by Audrey Wood (Scholastic, 1996). Readers meet Paul Bunyan's larger-than-life family, whose adventures lead them to carve out canyons, mountains, and waterfalls across America.

Cut From the Same Cloth: American Women of Myth, Legend, and Tall Tale by Robert D. San Souci (Philomel, 1993). Tall tales about familiar and little-known female heroes are featured in this entertaining collection.

John Henry by Julius Lester (Dial Books, 1994). Evocative illustrations enhance this stirring retelling of the famous contest between John Henry and the steam drill. A Caldecott Honor winner.

Sally Ann Thunder Ann Whirlwind Crockett: A Tall Tale by Steven Kellogg (William Morrow, 1984). Students will love reading about Sally Ann's amazing and outlandish adventures in this rollicking tale. Other titles in this series include *I Was Born About 10,000 Years Ago*, *Mike Fink*, *Paul Bunyan*, and *Pecos Bill*.

Swamp Angel by Anne Isaacs (Dutton, 1994). The author tells a story of her own invented tall tale character, the irrepressible Angelica Longrider from Tennessee. Vibrant, primitive-style paintings bring the Smoky Mountain setting to life.

A Note About the Plays in This Book

The tall tale plays in this book were adapted from a variety of sources. Because of the word-of-mouth nature of tall tales, story details vary from source to source. Details were chosen that seemed most common to all versions of a tale and that were interesting and appropriate for the elementary school audience.

Stormalong

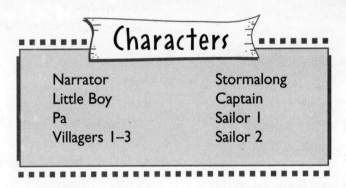

Characters

Narrator	Stormalong
Little Boy	Captain
Pa	Sailor 1
Villagers 1–3	Sailor 2

Narrator: One day, a big storm swept through a small village on the coast of Maine.

Little Boy: Pa, come quick! You won't believe your eyes!

Pa: What is it, son?

Little Boy: A big wave washed a baby up on the shore!

Pa: That's strange. A baby, huh?

Villager 1: Washed up on the beach?

Villager 2: You don't say!

Villager 3: Never heard of such a thing!

Little Boy: Yes, but...

Pa: But what?

Little Boy: Take a look! That baby is bigger than a house!

(Stormalong enters, looking as big as possible.)

Pa: Well, I'll be. Look at that. I'll bet folks here have never seen anything like this before.

Villager 1: Nope.

Villager 2: Sure haven't.

Villager 3: I'll say.

Little Boy: Can we keep him, Pa?

Pa: Well, it'll be hard to feed such a big baby, but okay.

Little Boy: He needs a name. How about Alfred Bulltop Stormalong?

Pa: That's a mighty big name, son.

Little Boy: We can call him Stormy for short, since he came to us during a storm.

Pa: Great idea. Stormy it is!

(All exit except Narrator.)

Narrator: Twelve years passed. Stormy went to school in the village. But he wasn't happy.

(Pa and Stormy enter.)

Pa: My word, Stormy. You've certainly grown into a fine young lad. All 36 feet of ya'!

Stormalong: Pa, people stare at me all the time.

Pa: Well, that's just because you're so handsome.

Stormalong: Nah, you know why. I'm bigger than a whale. I think it's time I moved somewhere else.

Pa: What do you have in mind?

Stormalong: I came from the sea and I belong on the sea. I'll become a sailor.

(Pa exits. Stormalong hikes around the stage.)

Narrator: So Stormalong set off to become a sailor. Soon he came upon a big ship.

(Captain and Sailors enter.)

Stormalong: Captain, sir?

Captain: Well, blow me down!

Stormalong: I'm looking for work. Can you use another sailor?

Captain: Well, you're a big boy, but I'm sure we could use ya'. Come aboard.

Sailor 1: Captain, you sure 'bout this?

Sailor 2: Yeah, he might sink the ship.

Captain: He's a fine lad. And he may come in handy someday.

Narrator: That day came soon after the ship set sail.

Sailor 1: Whoa! The sea is mighty rough!

Sailor 2: I think something's got hold of the ship! It's pulling us under!

Stormalong: Let me take a look.

(Stormalong pantomimes going into the water.)

Narrator: Stormy eased himself gently into the water. He didn't want to make a tidal wave!

Stormalong: It's a giant octopus. He's got all eight legs wrapped around our ship!

Captain: Can you help us, Stormy?

Stormalong: I've got an idea.

(Stormalong pantomimes swimming as he exits.)

Narrator: And Stormy disappeared under the water.

Sailor 1:   He's been under a long time.

Sailor 2:   I hope nothing's happened to good ol' Stormy.

Captain: Give him time. Stormy won't let us down.

(Stormalong enters, panting.)

Narrator: Sure enough, Stormy was soon huffing and puffing as he dragged himself back on deck.

Sailor 1:   What happened, Stormy?

Sailor 2:   What did ya' do?

Stormalong: Well, I tied all eight of those octopus legs into knots. By the time he gets himself untangled, we'll be long gone.

Captain: Great work, Stormy!

Narrator: Stormy worked on this ship for quite a while. But he still wasn't completely happy.

Sailor 1: What's wrong, Stormy?

Stormalong: Well, I don't mean to complain, but this ship is feeling too small for me. I might have to move along.

Sailor 2: But you can't. You're the best sailor this ship has ever seen!

Captain: I have an idea.

(Captain and Sailors pantomime building a big ship.)

Narrator: So the crew got to work. They built the biggest ship anyone's ever seen. That ship was so big that sailors had to ride horses just to get from one side to the other.

Captain: How's this, Stormy?

Stormalong: It's perfect. I can't thank you enough.

Sailor 1: I suppose you'll need a crew.

Stormalong: Well, I couldn't ask for a better crew than you fellas.
What do you say?

Sailor 2: Sure thing, Stormy!

Captain: We'd be honored to work aboard your vessel.

Narrator: Nowadays, sailors wear the initials A.B.S. on their uniforms. Most folks think that means "Able-Bodied Seaman." But we all know it stands for Alfred Bulltop Stormalong, the greatest sailor on the seas!

THE END

Teaching Activities

Stormalong

About This Tall Tale Play

Stormalong was first introduced in a song sung by working sailors. Sailors also told tales about this larger-than-life sailor. In 1930 an author named Frank Shay collected and retold the Stormalong tales and published them in his book *Here's Audacity*. Later, more Stormalong tales appeared in a pamphlet by C. E. Brown.

The ships on which Stormalong sailed—great wooden ships known as clippers—began sailing in the 1840s. They sailed from the United States around the world, importing and exporting goods. At that time, clipper ships were known as the fastest ships in the world. By the end of the Civil War, however, steamships and then oil-burning ships drove clippers off the seas.

Talk About the Play

- Why did Stormalong become a sailor?

- How did the sailors feel about Stormalong when they first met him? Why did they feel that way?

- What did Stormalong do to gain the sailors' trust?

- How did the crew and captain feel about Stormalong at the end of the play? What did they do to show their feelings for him?

13

What Happened First?
(Writing)

The play explains that Stormalong washed up on the shores of Maine during a storm. Ask your students to imagine what happened before that storm. What did Stormalong look like as a baby? What did he eat? What did he do? Who were his parents? How did he come to be washed ashore during a storm? Encourage students to write the beginning of Stormalong's tale in story or play form. Let those who write in play form add their scenes to the existing play and read aloud the extended version or act it out for the class.

I'm Thinking of a Creature ...
(Science)

Stormalong and the crew encountered a giant octopus during their travels. In fact, they may have come across a great variety of sea life. Encourage your students to research five of their favorite sea creatures and create a fact card for each one, writing three facts about the creature on one side of the card and drawing a picture of the creature on the other. Then divide the class into pairs. Encourage each pair to use their cards to play a sea creature guessing game. Here's how:

1. Player A reads one clue aloud to Player B.

2. Player B tries to guess the identity of the sea creature. If Player B guesses the creature based on one fact, he or she earns 10 points. If Player B guesses the creature in two clues, he or she earns 7 points. By guessing in three clues, he or she earns 5 points.

3. Encourage players to record scores and switch roles after each correct guess. Have them add up their points to see which player finishes with the highest score. Note: After students play in pairs, you may want to combine their cards to make a class set that students can use during free time.

How Big Was It?
(Writing, Art)

In tall tales, bigger is better and enormous is best of all. Stormalong's sailors built their hero a ship that was so big they "had to ride horses just to get from one side to the other." Search the play for other examples of exaggeration. Then let your students test their skills at stretching the truth. Invite them to write tall tale statements about their homes or possessions, such as "My backpack is so big I have to climb down inside it to get my lunch." Have students illustrate their tall tale statements, and display them in the classroom.

Johnny: Sir, what kind of gizmo is that? What's it doing?

Farmer: It's an apple press, Johnny. It presses the juice out of the apples to make apple cider.

Johnny: Look at all those apple seeds coming out the bottom!

Farmer: Yup. I'll keep a few to plant here and there. The rest I just throw away.

Johnny: May I have them?

Farmer: The seeds? Sure, I guess so. But what do you want some piddling ol' apple seeds for?

Johnny: I think I've found what I was meant to do.

(chanting)   Apples are good.
Apples are sweet.
Apples are so good to eat.
Apple trees grow
So tall in the sun.
I'll plant apple trees
For everyone!

Nathaniel: And that's how John came to be called Johnny Appleseed. His horse felt better, so the two of them set out again. Johnny met many people along the way.

(Johnny, still wearing the pot, sets out again, this time with a bag of seeds slung over his back.)

Johnny: Hello, friends!

Hannah: Pa, there's a strange man here. He's barefoot and he's got a pot on his head!

Father: Can I help you, stranger?

Johnny: No sir, but I'd like to help you. Here, take these apple seeds. Plant them and soon you'll have an apple orchard. You'll have apples for

jam, apples for pies, and just plain juicy apples for eatin'.

Father: What's the catch?

Johnny: No catch, sir. Just be kind to people and animals and the land will be kind to you, too.

Hannah: Take the seeds, Pa. Apples are yummy!

Father: Thank you, kind friend. Tell me, what is your name?

Johnny: Folks call me Johnny Appleseed.

Hannah: Thank you, Johnny Appleseed!

(Johnny continues on. Two Miami Indians are sitting on a log.)

Nathaniel: Johnny continued on his journey, giving apple seeds to people he met. Then he came upon two Miami Indians who were sitting by a river.

Johnny: Hello, friends! I'm Johnny Appleseed.

Miami Indian 1: We have heard of you.

Miami Indian 2: You are good to the land and its creatures.

Johnny: Would you trade some apple seeds for a canoe? I sure would like to cross this river so I can give away more of my apple seeds.

Miami Indian 1: We do not need apple seeds. We do need a horse.

Miami Indian 2: We will trade you our canoe for your horse.

Johnny: Hmm. Don't know 'bout that.

Miami Indian 1: Your horse will be treated with kindness.

**Miami
Indian 2:**   We, too, love the earth's creatures.

Johnny: Well, I sure will miss the ol' girl. But I can't take her in a canoe. And she does seem happy here.

Nathaniel: So Johnny traded the horse for a canoe. He made his way across the rough water. Johnny continued traveling west. He met many people along the way.

(Johnny pantomimes rowing a canoe over rough water. He gets out of the canoe and approaches two children as he chants.)

Johnny: Apples are good.
Apples are sweet.
Apples are so good to eat.

Timothy: Look! It's Johnny Applesauce!

Sarah: It's Johnny Apple*seed*, silly. Hello, Mr. Appleseed. We've heard about you. Did you bring us some seeds?

Johnny: I sure did. You be sure to plant these now, hear? Soon you'll have beautiful apple trees.

Wolf: HOOOOWWWL!

**Timothy
and Sarah:**   What's that?

Johnny: Sounds like a wolf in trouble. Poor thing. I gotta help that critter.

Timothy: Be careful, Johnny! Thanks for the seeds!

(Children exit. Johnny pantomimes climbing up a mountain.)

Nathaniel: So Johnny went up a mountain toward the howling.
He found a wolf caught in a trap.

Wolf: HOOOOWWWWL!

Johnny: Let me help you.

Nathaniel: Johnny undid the trap. The wolf licked Johnny's hand to thank him.

Johnny: You sure are welcome. Well, good-bye friend.

Nathaniel: But that wolf didn't want to leave Johnny. He followed him around just like a pet dog.

Johnny: Okay, friend. I can use the company. Let's be on our way.

Nathaniel: And that's how my brother spent his life. He gave away apple seeds for people to plant. He also planted a bunch himself. Soon the land was filled with apple orchards.

(Johnny addresses the audience.)

Johnny:
(chanting)

I've lived my dream.
My work is done.
There are plenty of apples for everyone.

This great land
Will be greater still,
As long as folks have dreams and goodwill.

THE END

Teaching Activities

Johnny Appleseed

About This Tall Tale Play

Johnny Appleseed's real name was John Chapman. While there is controversy over certain details of his life, people do agree on some facts. He was born in 1774 or 1775 in Massachusetts. Orphaned as a young boy, Chapman eventually traveled south to New York and New Jersey. He worked on a farm in Lancaster, Pennsylvania, and then moved on to Ohio, Indiana, and Illinois, where he began planting apple orchards in the wilderness. Chapman is well known for his kindness to people and animals as well as his eccentric lifestyle, which included walking barefoot and living in barns, livestock pens, and outdoors.

Talk About the Play

- What was Johnny's dream?
- How did Johnny think planting apple seeds would help the settlers?
- What are some ways Johnny suggested the settlers use apples? In what other ways do people use apples?

- Why do you think some people call Johnny Appleseed an American hero? Do you believe he is a hero? Why do you feel that way?

- What qualities in Johnny Appleseed do you admire? How might you use those in your life?

 Explore More!

Welcome, Johnny!
(Writing)

Invite students to imagine that Johnny Appleseed has come to their community. What would they say to him? What might he say back? Encourage students to write a short play to show what might happen. Let them work individually, in pairs, or in small groups. Invite groups or individuals to share their play with the class, assigning roles as needed. Compare their plays. How are they the same? How are they different?

And the Winner Is...
(Math)

Johnny Appleseed would be pleased with the wide variety of apples available these days! Conduct an apple survey in your class. (Check for food allergies beforehand.) Have several varieties of apples on hand (Macintosh, Red Delicious, Granny Smith, and so on). Cut each into small pieces and place on a plate, next to a whole apple of the same type. Label each apple and place an empty bowl behind it. Let students taste each kind of apple. Then have them write their name on a slip of paper and drop it in the bowl behind their favorite apple. Tally, graph, and discuss the results. Which apple was the class favorite? Were any two equally popular?

Speaking of Similies
(Language Arts)

Nathaniel Chapman described his brother Johnny as being "as real as the crunch of a ripe apple." Talk with your students about what Nathaniel meant by this. Help them to understand that a simile is a comparison of two unlike things, using the words *like* or *as*. Many tall tales rely on simile to paint a vivid picture of characters, scenery, or objects in the story. Give students practice at using similes. As a class or in small groups, students can think of similes to describe the following: a cold drink of water, a hot summer day, a speeding race car, a bumpy road, and a snarling dog.

John Henry

Characters

Preacher	Lucy
Ma	John Jr.
Pa	City Person
Steel Drivers 1–4	Country Person
John Henry	Country Folk
Steam Drill Salesperson	City Folk
Boss	

(Preacher talks to the audience.)

Preacher: Hear that train? Whenever I hear a train whistle, I think of John Henry. He drove steel spikes into mountains, to help make tunnels so trains could run right through. I remember the night John Henry was born.

Ma: What a beautiful baby. Let's name him John Henry.

Pa: He's a fine son, my dear. Don't you agree, Preacher?

Preacher:
(to parents) Well, I've never seen anyone like him.

(to audience) And I hadn't either. His arms were as thick as trees. His shoulders were as broad as a boulder. And this I wouldn't believe if I hadn't seen it myself . . . he was born with a hammer in his hand.

Ma: What's this? It looks like a hammer.

Pa: Now, where'd he get a thing like that?

Preacher:

(to parents) Looks like John Henry will be a steel-driving man.

(to audience) And that's just what he grew up to be. John Henry became the best steel driver in the land. In fact, he could do the work of four steel drivers put together.

Steel Driver 1: Boy, I'm beat.

Steel Driver 2: Me, too.

Steel Driver 3: I gotta rest.

Steel Driver 4: Right now.

John Henry: Can I help you fellas?

Steel Driver 1: Aren't you tired too, John Henry?

John Henry: Nah. I love my work and it comes easy to me. I was born with a hammer in my hand and I'll die the same way!

Steel Driver 2: I sure do wish I had your energy.

Steel Driver 3: We sure do appreciate your help.

Steel Driver 4: Thanks a lot.

John Henry: Well, a man ain't nothing but a man. He's just got to do his best.

Preacher: John Henry finished all the work for them in no time. One day a salesperson came to town.

(Salesperson enters with City Folk.)

John Henry: What is that huge piece of metal?

Salesperson: Step right up! Come see the greatest invention of all time—the steam drill! This baby can drive steel faster than three people!

Boss:	I've got a worker who can beat that, mister. What do you say we make a bet. If my man beats your machine, I get the machine for free. If he doesn't, I'll buy it from you.
Salesperson:	Deal!
Boss:	John Henry, do you think you can do it?
John Henry:	Well, I reckon I can—if I can use two hammers, one in each hand.
Preacher:	John Henry's wife was there that day visiting with their son, John Jr. Lucy didn't like what she heard.
Lucy:	Don't be a fool, John Henry.
John Jr.:	Will you do it, Pa?
John Henry:	Son, I can't stand the thought of machines taking the place of good, hardworking people. I've got to prove that people are worth more than machines.
Lucy:	Well, I don't want to see you get hurt. Come on, John Jr. We'll wait for your Pa at home. Be careful, John Henry.
Preacher:	So the race was on. The steam drill took off much faster than John Henry. Soon it was in the lead.
City Person:	That machine will win in no time!
Country Person:	Just give John Henry time. You won't believe your eyes.
Preacher:	Sure enough, John Henry began gaining on the machine. Soon he was ahead. Sweat was pouring down his forehead like a waterfall.
Country Folk:	Go, John Henry!
City Folk:	Go, steam drill!
Preacher:	Suddenly the crowd heard the machine sputter and choke.

Boss:	Looks like I won the bet, friend. But all I won is a broken machine.
Country Folk:	Hooray for John Henry! Hooray!
Salesperson:	Fair enough. John Henry is amazing. And look! He's still going strong!
Boss:	Okay, John Henry, you can stop. The race is over.
John Henry:	Just a bit more, Boss. I can make it through this mountain.
Preacher:	Well, just as John Henry cleared a pass right through the mountain, he fell down and died.
Boss:	John Henry always said he was born with a hammer in his hand and he'd die the same way.
Preacher:	So next time you hear a train whistle, do what I do. Think of John Henry. And think of how he helped to tunnel a way through the mountains so America could grow.

THE END

Teaching Activities

John Henry

About This Tall Tale Play

Historians disagree about whether John Henry was a real man. He may have been a newly freed slave hired by the Chesapeake & Ohio Railroad Company after the Civil War. The company laid down hundreds of miles of railroad track through West Virginia, hiring steel drivers to blast tunnels through the Allegheny Mountains. To blast through, the drivers drilled steel spikes into the mountain rock to make holes. Then they packed the holes with dynamite. This was a dangerous job, and many workers died performing it.

Based on the character John Henry may have sung work songs sung by railroad workers. Singing helped the workers get through their hard tasks. Whether John Henry was real or not, he became an inspiration to African American laborers and others as well.

Talk About the Play

◆ In what ways was young John Henry different from most babies?

◆ Did John Henry like driving steel? What parts of the play tell you this?

- What do you think John Henry meant when he said, "Well, a man ain't nothing but a man. He's just got to do his best"?

- John Henry wanted to prove that people are worth more than machines. Why was that so important to him? Do you agree with John Henry? Why or why not?

 Explore More!

Ready, Set, Work!
(Math, Social Studies)

John Henry believed that human workers are better than machines. Test this belief with your class. As a class, create a list of machines your students would like to compete against, in school or at home (for example, an electric mixer, an electric pencil sharpener, a dishwasher, an electric can opener), and design ways to test them. Have students compete, and then come together as a class to discuss their findings. Did any students perform better than machines? (in time, in quantity, in quality, and so on) If so, invite them to write tall tales about the experience. Did any machines outperform students? If so, remind the class that John Henry's story is a tall tale—many of its details are exaggerated. In reality, machines are designed to make tasks easier; many surpass human speed and ability.

What's in Your Hand?
(Writing, Art)

John Henry was born with a hammer in his hand. Based on that, the preacher predicted John Henry would be a steel driver when he grew up. Apply this connection to your students. Ask what they'd like to be when they grow up. Then invite them to pretend that, like John Henry, they were born holding an object that relates to their future. What would it have been? Invite students to draw a picture of themselves holding that item and to write a paragraph telling why they are holding it.

Create a Character
(Writing, Art)

The preacher said that John Henry's arms were "as thick as trees" and his shoulders were "as broad as a boulder." Have your students draw a picture of John Henry with these images in mind. Then invite them to create their own legendary character, using two or three similes to describe the character's body shape, size, or appearance. You might have students go beyond the exercise and give life to their characters in story or comic strip form.

Sally Ann Thunder Ann Whirlwind

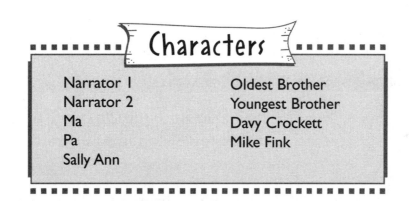

Characters

Narrator 1
Narrator 2
Ma
Pa
Sally Ann

Oldest Brother
Youngest Brother
Davy Crockett
Mike Fink

(Although it is said that the family has nine sons, only two have lines. You may choose to have seven actors standing onstage, or simply have the two who speak.)

Narrator 1:   A long time ago, a baby girl was born in Kentucky.

Narrator 2:   Her parents already had nine sons. They were happy now to have a daughter.

Ma: She's got a smile like a sunrise.

Pa: What should we name her?

Sally Ann: I'm Sally Ann Thunder Ann Whirlwind!

Ma and Pa: You can talk!

Sally Ann:	Why sure. I can outtalk, outrun, and outswim any baby in Kentucky!
Ma:	That's our girl!
Pa:	She's a whirlwind, all right!
Narrator 1:	Sally's parents were very pleased with her.
Narrator 2:	But her brothers weren't. They were hoping for another brother.
Oldest Brother:	She's just telling fibs. Everyone knows babies can't run.
Youngest Brother:	Especially baby girls.
Sally Ann:	Hey, let's race to the top of the mountain!

(Sally races offstage. Brothers follow more slowly.)

Narrator 1:	Sally ran up the mountain and back. By the time her brothers got to the top, Sally Ann was already back home having a bottle.

(Sally returns onstage, pantomimes drinking from a bottle. Brothers come back onstage. They are out of breath.)

Narrator 2:	When she was done, she felt like swimming.
Sally Ann:	Well, who's up for a swimming race?
Oldest Brother:	Not me. I'm beat.
Youngest Brother:	You go on ahead.

(Sally Ann pantomimes jumping into water and playing with otters.)

Narrator 1:	Sally Ann jumped into the water. Soon she was playing with otters.

(Sally Ann pantomimes juggling fish in the water.)

Narrator 2: When her brothers saw her juggling some fish, they had to admit she was something special.

Sally Ann: Fire up the griddle, Ma. It's time for a fish fry!

Oldest Brother: I guess she's okay.

Youngest Brother: For a girl.

Sally Ann:
(to audience as she "gets out of the water")
A girl that can outwrestle, outjump, and outholler anyone in town!

Narrator 1: Sally Ann grew and grew. When she was about ten, she decided to go live in the woods.

Sally Ann:
(to audience) I needed some new challenges.

Narrator 2: She chewed trees with beavers. She hibernated with bears.

Narrator 1: She wore a beehive as a hat and put on skunk perfume.

Narrator 2: She lived out there for ten years. One day, she heard a man yelling.

(Davy Crockett enters. He pantomimes being stuck in a tree.)

Davy: Help! Somebody, help me!

Sally Ann: Looks like you're stuck in a tree, partner.

Davy: That I am, little lady. The name's Davy Crockett. Maybe you can give me a hand.

Sally Ann: One, I'm not little. And two, I'm not just a lady. I can outkick, outyell, and outsmart any man around. But I guess I'll help you. The name's Sally Ann.

(Sally Ann looks down and pantomimes finding six rattlesnakes, tying them together, and lassoing Davy out of the tree.)

31

| **Narrator 1:** | Sally Ann found six rattlesnakes. She tied them together and lassoed Davy right out of that tree. |

(Davy "jumps" down onto the ground.)

| **Davy:** | Wow! Much obliged, ma'am. |

| **Narrator 2:** | After that, Davy and Sally became great friends. Soon they were married. They lived in a simple log cabin. |

| **Narrator 1:** | Once, while Davy was away, Sally heard noises on the roof. |

| **Sally Ann:** | Now, what in tarnation can that be? |

| **Narrator 2:** | She looked on the roof and there were 20 alligators tap dancing! |

(Sally Ann pantomimes seeing the alligators.)

| **Sally Ann:** | Get off o' my roof, you varmints! |

| **Narrator 1:** | But the alligators didn't budge. |

(Sally Ann pantomimes wrestling with alligators.)

| **Narrator 2:** | So Sally Ann started wrestling with those alligators so hard that she made a giant tornado. |

(As she is wrestling, she looks up as though alligators are flying overhead.)

| **Sally Ann:** *(to audience)* | Those alligators flew so high in the sky, it rained alligators for a week! |

| **Narrator 1:** | Tough guy Mike Fink heard this story, but he didn't believe it. |

| **Mike Fink:** | No way a gal could be a match for alligators. I've got a plan to show people I'm right. |

| **Narrator 2:** | Mike dressed in an alligator costume and snuck up on Sally Ann one night. |

32

Mike Fink:	I'm going to get you!

| Sally Ann: | Outta my way, you rascal! |

| Narrator 1: | But Mike kept on trying to scare Sally Ann. |

| Mike Fink: | Boo! Boo! |

| Sally Ann: | Why you . . . |

(Sally Ann pantomimes swinging Mike by the tail. Both Mike and Sally spin around until she "flings" Mike offstage.)

Narrator 2:	She took Mike by the tail and swung him around so hard the costume flew right off and Mike landed in the river.

| Sally Ann: | That'll teach you to mess with Sally Ann Thunder Ann Whirlwind! |

| Narrator 1: | From then on, people everywhere respected Sally. |

| Narrator 2: | And no one ever tried to trick her again. |

| Sally Ann:
(to audience) | That's for sure! |

THE END

Teaching Activities

Sally Ann Thunder Ann Whirlwind

About This Tall Tale Play

Sally Ann Thunder Ann Whirlwind represents the women of the backwoods of Tennessee and Kentucky who struggled, along with their men, to make a life in the wilderness. The women who traveled with their families to settle this land helped to build cabins, clear land for planting, and perform many other arduous tasks.

Sally Ann is briefly mentioned in *Davy Crockett's Almanacks* as his fictional wife. (Davy Crockett was a real person, born on the frontier in 1786. He was a woodsman and soldier who served in Congress in the early 1800s.) The stories in the Almanacks also tell the tales of other strong female characters who, like Sally Ann, are rugged frontier women who perform amazing feats. One of these women was the real-life Sal Fink, daughter of Mike Fink, the legendary riverboat man who lived from 1770–1823. The exaggerated stories of the Fink family were popular in newspapers in the early 1800s.

Talk About the Play

- How did Sally Ann's brothers feel about her when she was born? Why did they feel that way? What happened in the play that caused them to change their feelings toward Sally Ann?

- What are some of the things Sally Ann felt she could do better than anyone?

- What do you think Davy Crockett admired about Sally Ann when he met her?

- Why did Mike Fink want to outsmart Sally? How did he try to outsmart her? What happened?

 Explore More!

Sharing Skills
(Language Arts)

Sally Ann had a lot of confidence in her ability to do many things well. Chances are, your students feel the same way about themselves regarding at least one skill. Gather in a circle and invite each student to state one thing he or she does well and one thing he or she would like to learn to do better. For example, a student might say, "I'm really good at drawing. I'd like to be better at ice-skating."

Extra! Extra!
(Writing)

Invite students to write newspaper articles about how Sally Ann rid her home of the alligators, how she outsmarted Mike Fink, or any other newsworthy aspect of her life. First, bring in newspapers so students can study the format. Then try the following:

- Point out that most news articles have headlines that sum up the story. Review headlines from local papers. Let students suggest headlines that might go with stories about school events, such as an upcoming bake sale or a recent class trip. Then move on to a Sally Ann topic. Headline ideas may include "Sally Ann Makes It Rain Alligators!" or "Mike Fink Is No Match for Sally Ann."

- Let students work individually, in pairs, or in small groups to write Sally Ann stories and create headlines, pictures, and captions to go with them.

- If possible, present each story on a mock newspaper page. Many computer programs provide news-style fonts that will create an authentic look.

Exaggeration Station
(Writing, Language Arts)

Take your students one—or 20!—step beyond reality. Experiment with exaggeration, a key element in tall tales. Sally Ann wrestled 20 tap-dancing alligators and caused a tornado, all on the roof of her house. What unusual feats can your students do in their spare time? Let students work independently to write or tell a brief but exaggerated tale of fun, heroism, or valor, with themselves in lead roles.

Annie Christmas

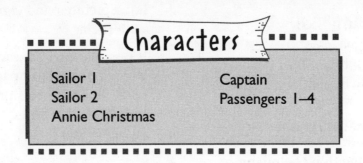

Characters

Sailor 1
Sailor 2
Annie Christmas

Captain
Passengers 1–4

Sailor 1:	Ha, ha!
Sailor 2:	What's so funny?
Sailor 1:	I was just thinking about Annie Christmas.
Sailor 2:	Oh, Annie. Yup, she was some gal.
Sailor 1:	All seven feet and 250 pounds of her!
Sailor 2:	But not everyone was fond of her.
Sailor 1:	No, siree. No man wanted to admit that a woman could be a better keelboat sailor than he was.
Sailor 2:	But she was the best.
Sailor 1:	I remember when we first met her.

(Annie enters.)

Annie: Hello, sailors.

Sailor 2: Evenin' ma'am.

Sailor 1: Say, what's with that necklace you're wearing? It must be nearly 30 feet long!

Annie: Yup, and it may get even longer. I add a bead to it every time I whup a man in a fight.

Sailor 2: What? A pretty thing like you? You don't scare me.

Annie: Well, you may want to talk to that gentleman over there. He didn't believe me either.

Sailor 1: You mean the one on the ground with the black eye?

Annie: That's the one.

Sailor 2: Okay, we believe you.

Sailor 1: So where are you off to, dressed so fancy?

Annie: Well, I thought I'd treat myself to a night of dancing on your fine ship. I've tied my keelboat to the back.

(Captain enters.)

Captain: Well, who have we here?

Annie: Annie Christmas, Captain.

Captain: Annie Christmas! I've heard about you. Folks say you're the best keelboat driver in the South. Hard to believe.

Annie: Why is that so hard to believe?

Captain: No offense, ma'am, but you're a woman. And everyone knows a woman can't be the best.

Annie: You can believe what you want. I'm just here to have a good time on your boat tonight.

Captain: Well, okay, but I don't want no trouble, ya' hear?

Sailor 2:
(to audience) So began a night I'll never forget.

Sailor 1:
(to audience) Me, neither. Annie had a fun night, dancing and singing. Then the storm hit.

Annie: Looks like some storm coming through. We'd better turn around, Captain.

Captain: Listen here, lady. I'm the Captain of this ship and I say we keep going.

Annie: But we're heading for a thin channel. The boat will never fit through it!

Captain: I said I didn't want any trouble from you. Now go back to your dancing.

Sailor 2:
(to audience) The water was rough. The boat was tossing all over the place.

Sailor 1:
(to audience) Many of the other passengers were getting scared. So was I.

(Passengers and Sailors pantomime being on rough water.)

Passenger 1: The river's getting rough. I hope we're going back to shore!

Passenger 2: There's trouble ahead. The ship is going to ram right into those rocks!

Annie: Captain, the passengers are worried. I'm worried. Please, turn this boat around.

Sailor 1: Captain, sir, maybe the lady's right.

Captain: Sailor, if you want to keep your job, you'd better hush up.

Sailor 2: But Annie has a point. This boat's too big for that channel.

Captain: Go! All three of you! This boat's moving forward and that's that!

Annie: Sailors, I have an idea.

(to Passengers) Listen, all passengers! My keelboat is tied to this ship. I can take you all to safety. Now, who's coming?

Passenger 3: I am. Show me the way.

Passenger 4: I'm staying put. That boat is much smaller than this one. It will sink.

Passenger 1: Well, I'm going with Annie Christmas. She's the best keelboat driver on any river, anywhere!

Passenger 2: I'm with you. Is there room, Annie?

Annie: Plenty of room. But we've gotta go now! Sailors, are you with me?

Sailor 1:
(to Annie) Aye-aye, Captain Christmas!

(Passenger 4 and the Captain exit. The other Passengers, the Sailors, and Annie pantomime getting onto Annie's boat.)

Sailor 2:
(to audience) So off we went. Annie poled that keelboat like no one I've
ever seen. But the waves were strong. The boat was moving slowly.

Passenger 1: Annie, I'm afraid we're going too slow.

Passenger 2: We'll never make it to shore in time.

Annie: You're right. I'm going to tie this rope around my waist. Sailors, tie
the other end to the boat. I'm gonna walk this baby in.

*(Annie pantomimes tying a rope around her waist while the sailors pantomime
tying the other end to the boat. Annie walks ahead of the boat, as though
struggling in water.)*

Sailor 1:
(to audience) And that's what Annie did. She walked through the choppy river
and brought the boat safely to shore.

**Passengers
and Sailors:** YAY! HOORAY for Annie Christmas!

(All exit except Sailors, who speak to audience.)

Sailor 2: We never did see the Captain again.

Sailor 1: No, but we saw a lot more of Annie Christmas.

Sailor 2: Yup. We started working for her. We also became friends.

Sailor 1: I sure do miss her.

Sailor 2: But we'll always have great memories of Annie Christmas,
Queen of the Mississippi!

THE END

Teaching Activities

Annie Christmas

About This Tall Tale Play

The character of Annie Christmas was created in the 1920s by two newspaper writers in New Orleans. They were tired of tall tales they'd heard and decided to create their own. The people of New Orleans were so excited about this new character that they adopted her as a New Orleans heroine. Annie reportedly worked as a longshoreperson on the docks of the Mississippi River near the French Quarter in New Orleans. Her height and weight came in handy when dealing with bullies who occupied the docks.

Her strength became so renowned that the phrase "as strong as Annie Christmas" became a much-sought-after compliment!

Talk About the Play

◆ What made Annie Christmas different from most women?

◆ Why didn't the Captain think Annie could be a great keelboat driver? Do you agree or disagree with him? Why?

- Why wouldn't the Captain turn the boat around when the seas grew rough?

- Did the sailors trust Annie during the storm? How do you know this?

- Why did the sailors call Annie the "Queen of the Mississippi?"

 Explore More!

Tell Tales Together
(Language Arts)

Two sailors in the play act as narrators and take turns telling the details of Annie's story. Try this alternating technique with your class, all together or in small groups. Ask one student to start a story by saying one sentence aloud. Then have another student add a sentence to the story. Continue in this manner, as students create their own tall tale aloud. Encourage them to fill the story with tall tale elements such as exaggeration, metaphor, simile, and descriptive language. (You might appoint in each group a scribe— someone who records the narrative in writing or on tape, in case students want to act it out later.)

Earn Beads for Deeds
(Social Studies, Art)

Annie Christmas wore a necklace with a bead for each man she'd beaten in a fight. Since this is not a behavior to be encouraged, take the idea in a new direction with "Good Deed Bead" necklaces. To do this, you'll need string and a bucket of beads. Have each student cut a length of string to tie loosely around the neck. Each time the student does a good deed, he or she can add a bead to the necklace. (Those who don't wish to wear the necklaces can store them in a safe place where they are accessible for add-ons.) Incorporate the "Good Deed Bead" ritual into morning meetings, or designate a special time when students can share their good deeds with the class.

Extra! Extra!
(Writing)

To save the sailors, Annie tied a rope to her waist and pulled her keelboat to shore. Such superhuman feats are common in tall tales. Remind students of this, and ask them to recall other characters who have performed amazing acts in tall tales, in fiction, and on television. Make a chart to record the characters' names and their actions and/or contributions.

Febold Feboldson

Characters

Pioneer 1	Olaf Swenson
Pioneer 2	Anna Swenson
Febold	Frogs 1–4
Travelers 1–4	

Pioneer 1: When we first met Febold Feboldson, he lived on the Great Plains.

Pioneer 2: Febold was very lonely. He wanted other people to settle near him. Whenever travelers passed by he would yell out to them.

(Travelers 1 and 2 enter.)

Febold: Hey! Why don't ya' come live here!

Traveler 1: Can't. We're going to California.

Traveler 2: There's gold out there.

(Travelers 1 and 2 exit.)

Febold: Gold? Well, there's golden sunshine right here.

Pioneer 1: But the travelers were gone. Febold kept trying though, whenever anyone passed by.

(Travelers 3 and 4 enter.)

Febold: Hello! Stay here and settle down!

Traveler 3:   We're on our way farther west.

Traveler 4:   Gold's a-waitin' for us there!

(Travelers 3 and 4 exit.)

Febold: So, it's gold they want, huh?

Pioneer 2:   Febold had an idea.

Febold: If it's gold they want, it's gold they'll get.

Pioneer 1:   Febold ordered one thousand goldfish from far away.

(Febold pantomimes dumping goldfish into the lake.)

Pioneer 2:   He dumped them into the lake. This time, when travelers passed by, they stopped.

(Olaf and Anna enter.)

Olaf: There's gold here!

Anna: Quick! Get off the wagon and start panning.

Febold: It worked! Now I will have neighbors.

Pioneer 1:   Soon, more and more people arrived. They all wanted to get the gold that was shimmering in the lake.

Pioneer 2:   But soon they grew tired and hot.

Olaf: It's too hot and dry out here. And besides, there's no gold here— just goldfish.

Anna: We'd better move on and find a better place to live.

Febold: Wait! Please stay here tonight. I promise you some rain by tomorrow.

Olaf: What can you do to make it rain?

Febold: Oh, just leave that up to me.

(Olaf and Anna exit.)

Pioneer 1: But Febold really didn't know what he would do.

Pioneer 2: Febold thought and thought. Finally, he did a little dance. He had an idea!

Febold: I'll build a big fire near the lake. The heat will make the lake water rise into the air. Then it will rain back down!

Pioneer 1: The next day, Febold built a fire. Soon, big clouds formed above the lake. It began to rain!

(Olaf and Anna enter. They pantomime not being able to see through the fog.)

Pioneer 2: But the rain never hit the ground. The air was so hot and dry that the rain turned to steam. The steam turned to fog. Soon the settlers couldn't see.

Olaf: This is terrible!

Anna: Let's get out of here!

Febold: Wait! I can get rid of the fog!

(Febold pantomimes cutting through the fog with large scissors and burying it in the ground.)

Pioneer 1: Febold took out a big pair of scissors.

Pioneer 2: He cut the fog into strips and buried it in a field.

Olaf: Well, there's no more fog, but we can't live without rain.

Anna: Off to California we go!

Febold: Friends, please. I'll bring rain. Just let me think. Hmm . . . I know! We need noise!

**Olaf
and Anna:**   Noise?!

Febold: Sure. It always rains when there is a lot of noise. Fireworks, outdoor concerts, parties. What we need are some frogs.

**Olaf
and Anna:**   Frogs?!

Febold: Sure. Frogs make lots of noise.

(Febold gathers Frogs onstage. They sit quietly.)

Pioneer 1:   So Febold rounded up all the frogs on his farm. There were hundreds of them.

Pioneer 2:   The only problem was, frogs only make noise when they're wet and these frogs were very dry. Plus, the lake had dried up by now.

Febold: I know. I'll make them think it's raining. There's still one drop of water left in the well. That oughta do it!

(Febold pantomimes getting a drop of water from the well. He then "puts" the drop on Frog 1. Then he bends down low to whisper in the frog's ear.)

Pioneer 1:   Febold got the one drop of water from the well. He put it on one of the frogs. Then he whispered to that frog.

Febold:
(whispering)   Hey, froggy, it's raining. It's raining. Look at all that rain!

Frog 1:   Ribbit.

Pioneer 2:   Febold had the frog believing it was raining. Once that frog started making noise, so did all the others.

Frog 2:   Ribbit, ribbit.

Frog 3:   Ribbit, ribbit, ribbit.

Frog 4:   Ribbit, ribbit, ribbit, ribbit.

All Frogs:	RIBBIT! RIBBIT! RIBBIT! RIBBIT! RIBBIT!
Pioneer 1:	Soon it began to rain.
Pioneer 2:	The people were so happy.
Olaf:	It worked! What beautiful rain!
Anna:	Febold is our hero!
Olaf:	We'll stay here and settle down.
Anna:	It's a magical land, indeed.
Pioneer 1:	People stayed. And more and more people came.
Pioneer 2:	Febold taught us all he knew about farming the Great Plains. He had helped to settle a new frontier!
All Frogs:	RIBBIT!

THE END

Teaching Activities
Febold Feboldson

About This Tall Tale Play

Febold Feboldson was invented by a Nebraska lumber dealer named Wayne Carroll. Febold stories first appeared in several Nebraska newspapers and later in the "Nebraska Folklore" pamphlets, telling of deeds he performed on the Great Plains.

The Great Plains were the last American frontier to be developed in the 1800s. As pioneers traveled west toward gold in California and the rich soil of Oregon, they crossed a barren land riddled with dust storms and grasshoppers. Some wondered if it could be settled. Febold epitomizes the farmer of the Great Plains who created new ways to overcome such unfamiliar obstacles. (It should be noted, however, that prior to the pioneers' arrival, generations of Native Americans had thrived on the Great Plains.)

Talk About the Play

◼ Why did Febold want others to live nearby?

◼ Why didn't people want to live on the Great Plains?

- What was the first thing Febold did to try and get settlers to stay? Why did he do that?

- What did Febold do to make rain the first time? Why didn't his plan work?

- How did Febold eventually make rain?

- What did Febold mean when he said that fireworks, outdoor concerts, and parties bring rain? Do you believe that? Why do you feel that way?

- What kind of person was Febold? What parts of the play tell you this?

Explore More!

Let It Rain!
(Science)

Help your students create rain in a box. To do this, you will need:
- one clear plastic box with a clear lid
- small bowl
- water
- lamp
- sealable plastic bag
- ice cubes

1. Fill the bowl with water, and place it in one corner of the box. Ask students to imagine it is water from an ocean, river, or lake.

2. Place a lamp a few inches from the top of the box. Be sure it shines on the jar lid. Explain that the lamp is like the sun.

3. Let students guess what will happen in the box.

4. Wait one hour. Then check inside the box. Has anything changed? How? (Condensation will have formed inside the box, over the bowl.)

5. Fill the plastic bag with ice cubes. Place it on top of the box, as shown, and leave the lamp on.

6. Wait two hours. Let students look inside the box again. Has anything changed? (The  cold from the ice cubes causes it to "rain" inside the box.) Invite students to speculate: What might have happened if they had not put ice on top of the box?

Come to the Plains!
(Writing, Art)

Febold really wanted people to settle on the Great Plains. He tried many tactics to sell them on the idea. Today when people want to sell something, they advertise. Invite students to create ads for the Great Plains, using information from the play or researching further. Encourage them to stand in Febold's shoes and come up with strong selling points. Their ads may take the form of posters, pamphlets, TV or radio commercials, newspaper entries, and so on. Let each advertiser present his or her ad to the class. Discuss which ads were the most effective and why. Brainstorm ways to strengthen the ads to entice pioneers to give the Great Plains a try.

Pecos Bill and Slue-Foot Sue

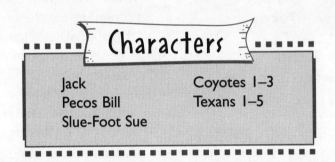

Characters

Jack	Coyotes 1–3
Pecos Bill	Texans 1–5
Slue-Foot Sue	

Jack:
(to audience) Howdy, folks. I'm here to tell you the story of my friend, Pecos Bill, and his wife, Slue-Foot Sue. When Bill met Sue, he was just a young lad throwing his lasso around a cactus, deep in the heart of Texas.

(Bill enters pantomiming swinging a rope above his head and lassoing a cactus.)

Bill: Hey, Jack! Watch this one!

Jack:
(to Bill) Great going, Bill! You sure know how to throw a rope!

Bill: Lots of practice, Jack. That's the name of the game.
(Bill looks in the distance.) Hey, what the . . . What's that out on the river?

Jack: Looks like some gal on a boat.

50

Bill: That's no boat. It's a catfish! That gal's riding a giant catfish!

(Sue enters from the direction in which Bill is looking.)

Sue: Howdy, boys!

Jack: Afternoon, ma'am. That's a nice fish you got there.

Sue: Thank you. Her name's Kitty. She takes me all up and down this here river. Hey, who's your friend?

Jack: Oh, this here's Bill. Pecos Bill. Say hello to the lady, Bill.

Bill: Uh . . . uh . . . um . . .

Jack:
(to audience) But Bill couldn't speak. This was the woman of his dreams!

(to Sue) Guess the cat's got his tongue. Or maybe the catfish!

Bill: Miss, would you marry me?

Jack: What?!

Sue: Well, sir, I hardly know you. But you look like a kind man. Is he a kind man?

Jack: The best there is.

Sue: Well, all right, then.

Bill: Yeeee-hah!

Jack:
(to audience) So Bill and Sue were married. They were the happiest people around. But then one day, Sue had her eye on Bill's horse.

Sue: That's a mighty fine horse.

Bill: That's Widowmaker.

Sue: Why'd you name him that?

Bill: Because when any other man rides him, he makes that man's wife a widow.

Sue: Well, I'm no man. Mind if I ride him?

Bill: Uh . . . uh . . . um . . . I promised Widowmaker that no one else would ever ride him but me. But sure, go right ahead.

Jack:
(to Bill)   Bill, are you crazy?

Sue: Thank you kindly.

(Sue pantomimes getting on a horse. She bucks around and "flies" offstage. She "bounces" back onstage for a second and then goes back offstage. This is all done while Jack is saying the following lines.)

Jack:
(to audience)   Well, that was a mistake. As soon as Sue got on Widowmaker's back, he bucked and kicked and off flew Sue, right up into the sky. She came right down, but her skirt was so bouncy, she bounced right back up and stayed there, stuck on the moon!

Jack:
(to Bill)   Would you look at that?

Bill: Hoooowwwwlllll!

Jack: What are you doing, Bill?

Bill: Jack, I'm so sad. The woman of my dreams is gone. It makes me wanna howl. Hoooowwwwlllll!

(Coyotes enter.)

Coyote 1:   Hoooowwwwlllll!

Coyote 2:   Hoooowwwwlllll!

Coyote 3:   Hoooowwwwlllll!

(Coyotes exit.)

52

Jack:

(to audience) After that day, coyotes always howled as a way of talking to one another.

(to Bill:) Well, guess there's nothing we can do.

Bill: No, sir. You're wrong. I'm going to lasso her down from there.

Jack:

(to audience) And that's just what Bill did.

(Bill pantomimes lassoing way up high. Sue comes bounding back onstage.)

Sue: Thank you, sweetie.

Jack: Bill and Sue lived happily after that. But not everyone was happy.

(Texans enter.)

Texan 1: Man alive. It's dry as a bone out here.

Texan 2: It's been months since we've seen rain.

Texan 3: My well's dried up. I'm so thirsty!

Texan 4: My crops are dying. We need some rain!

Texan 5: My chickens are laying eggs that are already fried!

Sue: Hey, Bill, I have an idea.

Bill: What is it, honeybunch?

Sue: Well, remember when I took that trip up to the sky and back?

Bill: Sure do.

Sue: Well, while I was up there, I noticed that there's a Big Dipper and a Little Dipper.

Bill: Yup. Those stars sure are pretty.

Sue: Not only are they pretty. Those dippers are filled with water.

Bill: So?

Sue: Grab your rope.

Bill: What for?

Sue: We're gonna rope those dippers.

(Bill and Sue pantomime holding a rope together and lassoing way up high and pulling down on the rope. They can grunt to indicate that it's hard work.)

Jack: Next thing I knew, Bill and Sue had lassoed the dippers and were pouring water over the whole state of Texas!

Texan 1:   Water!

Texan 2:   At last!

Texan 3:   We're saved!

Texan 4:   So are my crops!

Texan 5:   Thank you, ma'am.

(Coyotes enter.)

Coyotes: Hoooowwwwllll!

Bill: See, honeybunch, even the coyotes are thanking us.

Sue: You're all very welcome. Hey, let's celebrate with a big hoedown.

Bill: Great idea! Let's go!

(All exit except Jack.)

Jack: Well, we had us some party. Lots of dancing and singing. Sue and Bill had a great life together. I'd say they were a perfect match, wouldn't you?

THE END

Teaching Activities

Pecos Bill and Slue-Foot Sue

About This Tall Tale Play

Pecos Bill has long been known as one of the greatest cowboys around. His legends and those of his wife, Slue-Foot Sue, have spread throughout the West. Their adventures first appeared in print in 1923 from a writer named Edward O'Reilly. O'Reilly wrote about the pair for a magazine called *Century*. Pecos Bill appears in stories about other tall tale heroes as well, having adventures with both Paul Bunyan and Febold Feboldson.

Talk About the Play

- What was Sue doing the first time Bill and Jack saw her? Could she really have done such a thing? What does that tell you about the play?

- What other outrageous or exaggerated events took place in the play?

- What happened when Sue rode Widowmaker? How did she use this experience to help others?

- At the end of the play, Jack said he thought Sue and Bill were a perfect

match. Why did he feel that way? Do you agree? Why or why not?

 Explore More!

Constellation Creations
(Social Studies, Art)

Share with your students a book about constellations. Help them examine the shapes of constellations and the images with which they have been linked over the centuries. Some constellations, such as the Big Dipper and the Little Dipper, are made up of stars that can be joined in connect-the-dot fashion to form an easily recognized image. Other constellations, however, consist of only two or three stars, and their patterns are more difficult to discern.

Encourage students to create their own constellations with construction paper; crayons, pencils, or markers; and star-shaped stickers. On one side of the paper, have each student place several stars to form an imaginary constellation. (For example, two stars near each other may form the eyes on an animal's face. A column of three may outline the spine of a person.) Ask students to repeat the patterns on the other side of the paper, but this time they should connect the stars with pencil, crayon, or marker to form the images. Let students take turns displaying their unconnected constellations. Classmates can guess what each represents and then check the flip side to see if they are right!

Make a News-Flash Splash!
(Language Arts)

When Bill and Sue brought rain to Texas by tipping over the Big and Little Dippers, it must have been big news indeed. Invite your class to create a mock newscast of Bill and Sue's special feat. In preparation, ask students to watch part of a news broadcast at home or in school. Encourage them to take on a variety of roles in their newscast: news anchors, reporters, Pecos Bill, Slue-Foot Sue, Jack, and even the coyotes. Urge the anchor person(s) to launch the broadcast by introducing the story. Then reporters may take over, interviewing the characters and broadcasting live at the scene. Invite other students to ask the characters questions, as in a press conference.

Write Your Own Tall Tale
(Writing)

Invite your students to add to the legends of Pecos Bill and Slue-Foot Sue. Let them create their own outrageous or exaggerated episodes, featuring both characters and set in the past, the present, or the future.

Paul Bunyan

Characters

Narrator 1	Villager 1	Logger 1
Narrator 2	Villager 2	Logger 2
Ma	Paul	Cook
Pa	Babe	Foreperson

Narrator 1: Not too long ago, a baby was born in the state of Maine.

Narrator 2: But this baby was like no other baby you've ever seen.

Ma: Honey, we need more food for baby Paul.

Pa: More food? Already? That baby eats more than 20 people do.

Ma: I know. This morning he ate 50 eggs and a bathtub full of porridge.

Pa: And that beard! Even *I* don't have a beard. Whoever heard of a baby with a beard?

Ma: True. I have to comb it with a pine tree to keep it smooth. Still, we're lucky to have such a healthy son.

Pa: Yup, and he sure is strong.

Ma: He's a good boy.

(Villagers 1 and 2 enter.)

Villager 1: Hello. May we come in?

Pa: Sure thing.

Villager 1: Well, I hate to complain, but this morning the ground shook so much that all of my dishes broke.

Ma: I'm afraid that was caused by baby Paul rolling over in his cradle.

Villager 2: And another thing, when you give that baby a bath in the river, every time he splashes around, my house gets flooded.

Pa: Gee, we're very sorry about that.

Villager 2: Please, you must do something. That baby of yours is just too big.

(Villagers exit.)

Ma: They're right, honey. What can we do?

Pa: As much as we love baby Paul, he'll have to go live in the woods. I'll give him an ax and a fishing pole. He'll grow up to be a fine outdoorsman.

Narrator 1: So, with tears in their eyes, Paul's parents said good-bye to Paul.

(Ma and Pa escort Paul offstage.)

Narrator 2: Paul taught himself to find food in the woods. He grew to be about 20 feet tall!

(Paul enters, rubbing his stomach. Babe is off to one side. Paul hasn't seen her yet.)

Paul: Yum! That was the best dinner I've ever had. Hey! It's snowing. But that big pile of snow is bright blue. How odd.

(Babe enters.)

Babe: Maaa! Maaa!

Paul: What's that?

Babe: Maaa! Maaa!

Paul: Why, it's a big blue baby ox. The snow must have turned her blue with cold. What's wrong little babe?

Babe: Maaa! Maaa!

(Paul walks over to Babe.)

Paul: Have you lost your mama? Well, you can live with me. I'll call you Babe. We'll be great friends!

Narrator 1:   Paul and Babe did become great friends. Babe grew so big that a person would need a telescope to see from her head to her hind legs.

Narrator 2:   In those days, the forests were filled with trees. But soon people needed them to build houses and ships. The logging industry had begun.

Paul: Babe, I'm going to become a logger. That way I can help people.

(Paul takes out his ax and chops at some trees.)

Paul: There! Ten trees at once! Come on, Babe. Let's bring these trees out west and get them to the mill.

(Paul and Babe walk around a bit.)

Narrator 1: Paul and Babe walked to Minnesota in about a week. They stopped at the Big Onion River. They decided to send the logs down the river to the mill.

Narrator 2: But the river was too curvy to sail logs down it. So Paul tied Babe to the bank at one end of the river and had her pull hard until the river was straight!

(Paul and Babe pantomime this action.)

Paul: Atta girl! That's better. Hey, if I had some help, we could log twice as fast. I need some workers.

(Logger 1 enters.)

Logger 1: How about me?

Paul: Well, you look big and strong. Sure.

(Logger 2 enters.)

Logger 2: I'd like to work for you, too.

Paul: You're hired!

Narrator 1: Paul hired only loggers who were ten feet tall and very strong. Soon he had about 1,000 loggers working for him.

(Loggers exit.)

Narrator 2: But feeding 1,000 ten-foot-tall loggers, plus Paul and Babe, was a tough job for the camp cook.

(Cook walks up to Paul.)

Cook: Boss, I've got a problem. I don't have a pan big enough to make flapjacks to feed all these loggers.

Paul: I know! I'll make you a pan as big as an ice-skating rink.

Cook: But how will I grease this pan?

Paul: We'll ask 100 loggers to put grease on the bottom of their boots and skate all over the pan until it's covered.

Cook: Great idea! But I'd like to make pea soup for supper. I don't have a big enough pot.

Paul: Let's fill the lake with peas. I'll stir it up and we'll have soup for everyone.

(Cook exits. Foreperson enters.)

Foreperson: Boss, I have a problem, too. The loggers are complaining that they're too cold.

Paul: I know! I'll cut some of my beard off. Then we can knit scarves and gloves for everyone!

Foreperson: Sure thing! But the loggers are also really thirsty.

Paul: I'll just dig a few ponds. The loggers can drink from them.

(Foreperson exits.)

Narrator 1: Those ponds became America's Great Lakes!

Narrator 2: Paul and Babe continued to move across the country with their logging company.

(Paul and Babe walk around a bit.)

Narrator 1: Some folks say they are still in the woods of the Northwest. Others say they've gone as far north as the Arctic Circle.

(Paul and Babe exit.)

Narrator 2: But wherever they are, you can be sure that they're doing really BIG things!

THE END

Teaching Activities

Paul Bunyan

About This Tall Tale Play

In the late 1870s, loggers began cutting down the huge forests that covered New England, the Pacific Northwest, and the woods near the Great Lakes to make room for settlers. While they were working in the woods, the loggers told tales around the fire at night to pass the time. Most people believe that it was through these tales that the legend of Paul Bunyan was born. Eventually, the character of Paul Bunyan appeared in so many newspaper articles and pamphlets that his name became widely recognized by the American public. Today there exist many versions of Paul Bunyan tales, read and enjoyed by children and adults alike.

Talk About the Play

■ How did the villagers feel about baby Paul living in their town? How do you know this?

■ What did Paul's mother and father do to answer the villagers' complaints?

- Paul Bunyan wanted to help people. In what ways did he help them?

- Imagine that Paul and Babe are still in the world somewhere. Where might they be? What might they be doing?

 Explore More!

Track a Tree
(Science, Art)

Paul Bunyan spent his life among trees. How well he must have known them! Help your students take a closer look at trees. Divide the class into pairs. Give each pair a pencil, a sheet of paper, scissors, and a measuring stick. Go to an area where there are plenty of trees. Have each pair select a tree and then sketch and describe it on paper. Encourage children to note characteristics unique to their tree, such as a knotty trunk or twisted branches. Ask them to note details that mark their tree's location (next to the monkey bars, behind the flagpole, and so on). Show students how to measure their tree's circumference: Wrap a length of string around the tree at shoulder height. Cut the string where the two ends meet. Remove the string and measure. Back in the classroom, invite students to share what they've learned. Post their drawings and descriptions for all to see.

Make It BIG!
(Writing, Art)

Paul's mother said she had to comb her son's beard with a pine tree. What other objects might Paul have needed to help him with aspects of daily life such as meals, recreation, and hygiene? Invite students to work individually or in groups to create one object that Paul (or Babe) might use, such as a toothbrush, shoe, brush for Babe's fur, fork or spoon, bowl for Babe to eat from, and so on. Provide art supplies such as clay, construction paper, cardboard, craft sticks, and wood for the inventions. Invite students to find ways to incorporate their inventions into the play.

What's the Problem?
(Language Arts)

Problem-solving is easy in tall tales—you make up the answers as you go along! In Paul Bunyan, Paul creates a griddle, a pot of soup, and ponds of drinking water without breaking stride. Give your students tall tale practice at solving problems. As a class, brainstorm a list of problems early settlers might have faced, such as inadequate transportation, lack of food or water, and threats from wildlife. Ask each student to choose one problem and tell what Paul Bunyan's response might have been.

# Notes